Sustainable Investing

The Basics

By: Joe Pastore

Copyright © 2024 by Joe Pastore

All rights reserved. No part of this book may be used or reproduced by any means, graphic, electronic, or mechanical, including photocopying, recording, taping, or by any information storage retrieval system, without the written permission of the publisher except in the case of brief quotations embodied in critical articles and reviews.

CONTENTS

Introduction 1

Chapter 1: Investment Basics..2

Chapter 2: Sustainability and Impact Investing 27

Chapter 3: ESG 41

Chapter 4: Climate Tech and Decarbonization.........................61

Introduction

"Life is what happens when you are busy making other plans."

~ John Lennon

Hi, this is Joe Pastore. This book was designed to give you the tools to understand sustainable investments starting from the basics of investing. It includes advanced strategies such as: hedge funds, and alternative investments and finally on Sustainability & Impact.

I will discuss the future of investing the implications of Sustainable & Climate Tech investing. Now may be the best time in history to get involved in the market with these new trends.

"Twenty years from now you will be more disappointed by the things you didn't do than by the ones you did."

~ Mark Twain

CHAPTER 1

Investment Basics

"Don't gamble," Buy a good stock. Hold it till it goes up...and then sell it. If it doesn't go up, don't buy it!"

~ Will Rogers

There is as much wisdom as humor in this remark. Success in the stock market is based on the principle of buying low and selling high. Granted, one can make money by reversing the order—selling high and then buying low.

I am writing as a professional investment advisor, one who has enjoyed a certain degree of success over the past 40 years and would like to share with you the some of the lessons that I learned.

So let's start with the basics.

Chapter 1 - Investment Basics

WHAT IS INVESTING?

Investing is the way of growing money. While there are many different classifications of investments, the four major ones are: stocks, bonds, real estate, and cash. Some people might include crypto currency as well. For each of these we invest our money hoping to get back a positive return (more money than we invested). Let us start with that to keep it simple.

What is a stock?

A stock is an investment in a specific company. The **stock** of a corporation is all of the shares into which ownership of the corporation is divided. A single share of the stock represents fractional ownership of the corporation in proportion to the total number of shares. This typically entitles the stockholder to that fraction of the company's earnings, proceeds from liquidation of assets after discharge of all senior claims such as secured and unsecured debt.

What is a bond?

A bond is a loan you make to a company or government. Also known as a fixed income instrument that represents a loan made by an investor to a borrower. A bond could be thought of as an I.O.U. between the lender and borrower that includes the details of the loan and its payments.

Bonds are used by companies, municipalities, states, and sovereign governments to finance projects and operations. Owners of bonds are debt holders, or creditors, of the issuer. Bond details include the end date when the principal of the loan is due to be paid to the bond owner & the terms for variable or fixed interest payments made by the borrower.

Cash investments

Cash Investments include everyday bank accounts, high interest savings accounts and term deposits as well as cash.

Real Estate

Real estate is property made up of land and the buildings on it, as well as the natural resources of the land, water, and any additional mineral deposits. The term *real estate* means *real*, or physical, property. The Constitution initially restricted voting rights to only owners of *real estate* which demonstrates its importance as an asset class.

Cryptocurrency

Cryptocurrency is a digital currency where transactions are maintained using cryptography rather than a centralized authority.

Chapter 1 – Investment Basics

What is a stock index?

A *stock index* or *stock* market *index* is a measurement of a section of the *stock* market. It is computed from the prices of selected stocks (typically a weighted average). It is a tool used by investors and financial managers to describe the market, and to compare the return on specific investments.

The two biggest and most important stock indexes are the Dow Jones Industrial Average (referred to as the Dow) and the Standard and Poor's 500 Index (referred to as the S&P 500).

The Dow Jones Industrial Average® (The Dow®), is a price-weighted measure of 30 U.S. blue-chip companies. The index covers all industries except transportation and utilities.

The S&P 500® is widely regarded as the best single gauge of large U.S. equities. The index includes 500 leading companies and covers approximately 80% of available market capitalization. With a combined value of over $9.9 trillion.

Inflation - an increase in prices and fall in the purchasing value of money. $1 today is worth less than $1 tomorrow.

Sustainable Investing

Sustainable investing can be described as directing capital to companies that seek to combat climate change.

ESG

ESG is a system of evaluating investments by how they are managing their strengths and weaknesses – whether related to climate change, human capital management, supply chain issues, diversity, or other balance sheet issues.

Decarbonization

Decarbonization is the reduction or elimination of carbon dioxide emissions from a process such as manufacturing or the production of energy

Climate Tech

Climate Tech primarily addresses the challenges of **climate change**, including reducing greenhouse gas emissions, mitigating global warming, and adapting to the changing climate.

Clean Tech

Cleantech is a term that encompasses technologies and processes that have a reduced impact on the environment. It often emphasizes cleaner and more sustainable alternatives to traditional technologies.

Now that we have some basic definitions, I want to talk about a few basic strategies to get us started. Many of these ideas were first stated by Sir John Templeton and Warren Buffet.

10 Basic Rules for Investment

1 Invest for maximum total real (after-inflation) return
2 Invest – don't trade or speculate
3 Remain flexible and open-minded about types of investments
4 Buy low
5 When buying stocks, search for bargains among quality stocks
6 Buy value, not market trends or the economic outlook
7 Diversify. In stocks and bonds, as in much else, there is safety in numbers
8 Aggressively monitor your investments and don't panic
9 Learn from your mistakes
10 There's no free lunch

Chapter 1 - Investment Basics

1. Invest for Maximum Total Return

This means the return on invested dollars after taxes and after inflation. This is the only rational objective for most long-term investors. Any investment strategy that fails to recognize the effect of taxes, expenses and inflation fails to recognize the true nature of the investment environment. Let me give you a simple example. If you buy a house for $1,000,000, hold if for 10 years and then sell it for $1,100,000. Assuming you have to pay $50,000 in taxes and $75,000 in broker's fees, you did not make money or have a positive return. And that does not even take into account inflation meaning that the gross amount of $1,100,000 may have less purchasing power than the $1,000,000 you used to purchase the house 10 years earlier.

It is important that you protect your purchasing power. One of the biggest mistakes people make is putting too much money into fixed-income securities. Today's dollar buys only what 35 cents bought in the mid-1970s, what 21 cents bought in 1960, and what 15 cents bought after World War II.

U.S. consumer prices have risen virtually every year. If inflation averages 4%, it will reduce the buying power of a $100,000 portfolio to $68,000 in just 10 years. In other words, to maintain the same buying power, that portfolio would have to grow to $147,000— a 47% gain simply to remain even over a decade. And this does not even account for taxes.

2. Invest, don't trade or speculate

The stock market is not a casino, but if you move in and out of stocks every time they move a point or two, or if you continually sell short...; or deal only in options; or trade in futures...the market will be your casino. And, like most gamblers, you may lose eventually—or frequently.

You may find your profits consumed by commissions. You may find a market you expected to turn down turning up— and up, and up—in defiance of all your careful calculations and short sales. Every time a Wall Street news announcer says, "This just in," your heart will stop.

It is amazing how much better the relaxed, long-term owners of stock do with their portfolios than the traders do with their constant buying and selling. The relaxed investor is usually better informed and more understanding of essential values; he is more patient and less emotional; he pays smaller capital gains taxes; he does not incur unnecessary brokerage commissions.

3. Remain Flexible about different types of Investments

There are times to buy blue chip stocks, cyclical stocks, corporate bonds, U.S. Treasury instruments, and so on. And there are times to sit on cash, because sometimes cash enables you to take advantage of investment opportunities.

The fact is there is no one kind of investment that is always best. If a particular industry or type of security becomes popular with investors, that popularity will always prove temporary and — when lost — may not return for many years.

Having said that, I should note that, for most of the time, most of our clients' money has been in common stocks. A look at history will show why. From January of 1946 through June of 1991, the Dow Jones Industrial Average rose by 11.4% average annually—including reinvestment of dividends but not counting taxes—compared with an average annual inflation rate of 4.4%. Had the Dow merely kept pace with inflation, it would be around 1,400 right now instead of over 42,000, a figure that seemed extreme to some 10 years ago.

Look also at the Standard and Poor's (S&P) Index of 500 stocks. From the start of the 1950s through the end of the 1980s—four decades altogether—the S&P 500 rose at an average rate of 12.5%, compared with 4.3% for inflation, 4.8% for U.S. Treasury bonds, 5.2% for Treasury bills, and 5.4% for high-grade corporate bonds.

In fact, the S&P 500 outperformed inflation, Treasury bills, and corporate bonds in every decade except the '70s, and it outperformed Treasury bonds—supposedly the safest of all investments—in all four decades. I repeat: There is no real safety without preserving purchasing power.

4. Buy Low

Of course, you say, that's obvious. Well, it may be, but that isn't the way the market works. When prices are high, a lot of investors are buying a lot of stocks. Prices are low when demand is low. Investors have pulled back; people are discouraged and pessimistic.

When almost everyone is pessimistic at the same time, the entire market collapses. More often, just stocks in particular fields fall. Industries such as automaking and casualty insurance go through regular cycles. Sometimes stocks of companies like the thrift institutions or money-center banks fall out of favor all at once. Whatever the reason, investors are on the sidelines, sitting on their wallets. Yes, they tell you: "Buy low, sell high." But all too many of them bought high and sold low. Then you ask: "When will you buy the stock?" The usual answer: "Why, after analysts agree on a favorable outlook."

This is foolish, but it is human nature. It is extremely difficult to go against the crowd—to buy when everyone else is selling or has sold, to buy when things look darkest, to buy when so many experts are telling you that stocks in general, or in this particular industry, or even in this particular company, are risky right now.

But, if you buy the same securities everyone else is buying, you will have the same results as everyone else. By definition, you can't outperform the market if you buy the market. And chances are if you buy what everyone is buying you will do so only after it is already overpriced.

Heed the words of the great pioneer of stock analysis Benjamin Graham. "Buy when most people...including experts... are pessimistic, and sell when they are actively optimistic."

Bernard Baruch, advisor to presidents, was even more succinct: *"Never follow the crowd."*

So simple in concept. So difficult in execution.

5. Search for Bargains among Quality Stocks

Quality is a company strongly entrenched as the sales leader in a growing market. Quality is a company that's the technological leader in a field that depends on technical innovation. Quality is a strong management team with a proven track record. Quality is a well-capitalized company that is among the first into a new market. Quality is a well-known trusted brand for a high-profit-margin consumer product.

Naturally, you cannot consider these attributes of quality in isolation. A company may be the low-cost producer, for example, but it is not a quality stock if its product line is falling out of favor with customers. Likewise, being the technological leader in a technological field means little without adequate capitalization for expansion and marketing.

Determining quality in a stock is like reviewing a restaurant. You don't expect it to be 100% perfect, but before it gets three or four stars you want it to be superior.

6. Buy Value, not Market Trends or Economic Outlook

A wise investor knows that the stock market is really a market of stocks. While individual stocks may be pulled along momentarily by a strong bull market, ultimately it is the individual stocks that determine the market, not vice versa. All too many investors focus on the market trend or economic outlook. But individual stocks can rise in a bear market and fall in a bull market.

The stock market and the economy do not always march in lock step. Bear markets do not always coincide with recessions, and an overall decline in corporate earnings does not always cause a simultaneous decline in stock prices. So, buy individual stocks, not the market trend or economic outlook.

7. Diversify – There is safety in numbers

No matter how careful you are, you can neither predict nor control the future. A hurricane or earthquake, a strike at a supplier, an unexpected technological advance by a competitor, or a government-ordered product recall—any one of these can cost a company millions of dollars. Then, too, what looked like such a well-managed company may turn out to have serious internal problems that weren't apparent when you bought the stock.

So, you diversify—by industry, by risk, and by country. For example, if you search worldwide, you will find more bargains—and possibly better bargains—than in any single nation.

8. Aggressively Monitor your investments

Expect and react to change. No bull market is permanent. No bear market is permanent. And there are no stocks that you can buy and forget. The pace of change is too great. Being relaxed, doesn't mean being complacent.

Consider, for example, just the 30 issues that comprise the Dow Jones Industrials. From 1978 through 1990, one of every three issues changed—because the company was in decline, or was acquired, or went private, or went bankrupt. Look at the 100 largest industrials on Fortune magazine's list. In just seven years, 1983 through 1990, 30 dropped off the list. They merged with another giant company, or became too small for the top 100, or were acquired by a foreign company, or went private, or went out of business. Remember, no investment is forever.

Sometimes you won't have sold when everyone else is buying, and you'll be caught in a market crash such as we had in 1987. There you are, facing a 15% loss in a single day. Maybe more.

Don't rush to sell the next day. The time to sell is before the crash, not after. Instead, study your portfolio. If you didn't own these stocks now, would you buy them after the market crash? Chances are you would. So, the only reason to sell them now is to buy other, more attractive stocks. If you can't find more attractive stocks, hold on to what you have.

9. Learn from your mistakes

The only way to avoid mistakes is not to invest—which is the biggest mistake of all. So, forgive yourself for your errors. Don't become discouraged, and certainly don't try to recoup your losses by taking bigger risks. Instead, turn each mistake into a learning experience. Determine exactly what went wrong and how you can avoid the same mistake in the future. The investor who says, "This time is different," when in fact it's virtually a repeat of an earlier situation, has uttered   the four most costly words in the annals of investing.

The big difference between those who are successful and those who are not is that successful people learn from their mistakes.

10. There's no such thing as a free lunch

This principle covers an endless list of admonitions. Never invest on sentiment. The company that gave you your first job, or built the first car you ever owned, or sponsored a favorite television show of long ago may be a fine company. But that doesn't mean its stock is a fine investment. Even if the corporation is truly excellent, prices of its shares may be too high.

Never invest in an initial public offering (IPO) to "save" the commission. That commission is built into the price of the stock—a reason why most new stocks decline in value after the offering. This does not mean you should never buy an IPO.

Never invest solely on a tip. Why, that's obvious, you might say. It is. But you would be surprised how many investors, people who are well-educated and successful, do exactly this. Unfortunately, there is something psychologically compelling about a tip. Its very nature suggests inside information, a way to turn a fast profit.

And now one last bonus principal:

Do not be fearful or negative too often

For 100 years optimists have carried the day in U.S. stocks. Even in the dark '70s, many professional money managers—and many individual investors too—made money in stocks, especially those of smaller companies.

There will of course be corrections, perhaps even crashes. But over time, stocks go up… and up…and up.

When communism fell the sharply reduced threat of nuclear war, gave the U.S. and some form of an economically united Europe a glorious period of growth.

As national economies become more integrated and interdependent, as communication became easier and cheaper, business has boomed. Trade has grown and wealth has increased. And stock prices have risen accordingly.

Chapter 1 – Investment Basics

As the 21st century has experienced explosive growth.

Chances are that certain other indexes will have grown even more. Despite all the current gloom about a pending recession after Covid, people will have more money than ever before in history. And much of it will be invested in stocks.

And throughout this wonderful time, the basic rules of building wealth by investing in stocks will hold true. In this century or the next it is still "Buy low, sell high."

WARREN BUFFETT'S TOP 5 TIPS FOR INVESTING

Warren Buffett is one of the most successful investors in history. His nickname is the *"Oracle of Omaha."*

Buffett is the quintessential value investor. He shares a lot of insights during shareholder meetings and in his annual letter to shareholders. As such, it is pretty easy to understand Warren Buffett's investing philosophy.

Plus, since his holdings are so widely followed, you can check his portfolio anytime at the [CNBC Berkshire Hathaway Portfolio Tracker](#).

While over time he has thrown out a ton of different tidbits on investing, here are the top five investing tips Warren Buffett has given:

1. Cash Is King

Cash is a big deal to Warren Buffett, and he keeps a lot of it on hand at any given time. The reason? In Warren Buffett's words, he keeps a lot of cash on hand "so that we can both withstand unprecedented losses and . . . quickly seize acquisition or investment opportunities."

In his 2011 letter to shareholders, Buffett reprinted a note from his grandfather from 1939: "I have known a great many people who at some time or another have suffered in various ways simply because they did not have ready cash . . . I hope it never happens to you."

That is solid advice for personal finance. You always want to maintain an emergency fund for the unexpected, but you should also keep cash in your brokerage account ready to go so that you can buy things on the dip.

For example, if you had piles of cash waiting to invest when the financial crisis hit, you could have bought low and sold high, reaping huge 50% to 100% profits on your investment. However, if you had everything tied up in investments, you would have just suffered large losses.

2. Be Fearful When Others Are Greedy

One of Buffett's most famous phrases is, "Be fearful when others are greedy, and greedy when others are fearful." This great sentiment is very true of our stock market and investing system. Buffet likes to joke that stocks are the only things that people are happy to buy when they are more expensive.

The bottom line is that you should avoid the stocks that everyone is buying, as they probably are overvalued. Instead, look for the stocks that few people are paying attention to, check their fundamentals, & invest if it makes sense.

3. Dividends Are Your Friend

Buffett loves dividends, as do most value investors.

Dividends are a great perk to buying a company, as it usually shows that the company's finances are in good enough shape to support paying out its hard-earned money.

Buffett likes companies that have a long history of paying dividends, and even increasing them over time. A popular tracker of these type of stocks is the Dividend Aristocrats, which are companies that have increased their dividends over the last 25 years.

Plus, Buffett recently announced that there is a good chance that the total amount of dividends paid by his position in Coca-Cola will soon surpass what he paid for the stock. That is a great return on investment!

4. Always Buy Undervalued Stocks

Buffett is a big-time value investor, and always looks to buy undervalued stocks based on their intrinsic value.

He calculates the intrinsic value by looking at the company's fundamentals — at a minimum of over the last five years, sometimes longer. He looks a lot at return on equity, operating margins, and having little or no debt. He compares the company to its peer group, and likes to see if it is undervalued.

A key part of this is also looking for companies that have some type of monopoly, special trait or economic moat as he likes to call it that will enable it to be successful in the future. This could be technology (even though Buffett avoids tech stocks that he doesn't understand), or even management. All of these factors can contribute to intrinsic value.

5. Buy and Hold

Finally, Buffett is a true buy-and-hold investor. He holds his positions for a long period of time, and constantly reiterates this to his followers.

In fact, he has said that he likes to "buy and hold forever." And it is true, since he has owned many of his positions for over 20 years, which is eons in the investing world.

However, he has also said that this doesn't mean hold a company if the fundamentals have changed. Buffett constantly looks at his portfolio and if a company loses its edge or superiority, then he does sell or trim back his position.

He also is a huge believer in patience. Basically, don't trade, invest. Find companies you like, and wait for the right price. It has been said that Buffett has a list of hundreds of companies that he wants to invest in, but that he is waiting for the right price and opportunity.

The last time he went on a buying spree was the Great Recession in 2008, when stock prices tanked. He was able to scoop up deals and get in on prices that made him get great returns in the following years.

CHAPTER 2

Sustainability and Impact Investing

"It is hard to fail but it is worse never to have tried to succeed"

~ Theodore Roosevelt

Sustainability and Impact Investing. People often times use the terms interchangeably so what is the difference? They both were born out of the necessity to create positive social and environmental change while generating financial gains. While they are often used interchangeably, let's explore the real differences between them.

What is Sustainable Investing?

Sustainable Investing means different things to different people. One definition is *"a variety of approaches in the financial markets aimed at building long-term wealth and creating positive social change."* Another definition is, *"investors aim to achieve financial returns while promoting long-term environmental or social value."* A third definition is, *"It aims to generate superior returns by investing in companies whose management employs sustainable practices."* Finally, a fourth definition is, *"directing capital to companies that seek to combat climate change."*

I personally am not a fan of the last definition as that is more specifically related to Climate Tech or Decarbonization.

But as you can see, all these definitions have something in common. In order to achieve these returns, they all require criteria or parameters to evaluate different companies. The system they all use is called ESG. I will devote an entire chapter to ESG so I don't want to go into too much detail here but briefly, ESG evaluates companies based on environmental, social, and governance (ESG) criteria.

Sustainable investing is committed to long-term growth while avoiding investments in companies whose business practices are *unsustainable*. Sustainable investments seek to preserve the environment and achieve financial stability. They may take various forms, including;

- Water preservation, reclamation & purification
- Air Pollution removal or avoidance
- Vertical or Organic farming
- Investments in renewable energy
- Waste reclamation or conversion

I like to use the acronym WAFE which stands for Water, Air, Food and Energy.

Sustainable investing aims to create portfolios that provide financial stability and achieve positive long-term performance. Therefore, investors pick companies not just for their intrinsic value. They also consider the positive change they will bring to society.

In recent years some projects have gotten a bad name because they were implemented without focusing of financial gain. The reality is that as much as everyone wants a clean planet, investors will not usually write a check unless the returns are there. Designing projects without the corresponding financial rewards more often than not are doomed to fail.

A colleague of mine, Peter Fusaro, who is called the Godfather of Green', has been working on sustainability projects for over for 50 years. He has been running the Wall Street Green Summit, which is the oldest 'Green' conference in the United States for over 20 years. Peter coined the phrase, *'Environmental Investing with Alpha.'* So, keep that in mind when evaluating companies or projects. They must have comparable or better projected returns than projects that do not have a positive environmental impact. Just because a project, idea or company is doing the right thing for the environment does not mean it will attract the investors necessary to be successful.

Impact Investing
Like sustainable investing, impact investing is a methodology that aims to achieve positive social and environmental impact. Impact investing is a branch of or subset of sustainable investing.

Impact investors promote businesses and projects that improve society or the environment. Impact investing combines social goals with financial objectives. This way, they make financial institutions, corporations, governments, and non-profit organizations can implement meaningful, positive change in the world.

Impact investing can be used to develop projects that improve people's lives in underdeveloped countries as one example. It is a way of putting money to work for larger purposes for the community. As it goes with its name, impact investing aims to produce a positive *impact* on the world and the people in it. The following chart will help to highlight the differences between Sustainable Investing and Impact Investing.

	Sustainable Investing	Impact Investing
Primary Focus	Investing in companies with positive ESG practices	Investing in projects or companies that generate measurable social or environmental impact
Financial Returns	Aims to achieve market-rate returns while considering ESG factors	May accept below-market returns in exchange for greater impact
Impact Measurement	Impact is often a byproduct of the investment process	Impact is the primary goal and is actively measured and reported
Investment Approach	Typically focuses on public markets and traditional asset classes	Can include private markets, venture capital, and alternative asset classes
Investor Involvement	Investors may engage with companies to encourage better ESG practices	Investors often work closely with investees to ensure impact goals are met
Examples	Investing in a stock fund that screens for companies with low carbon emissions	Investing in a microfinance institution that provides loans to underserved communities

Types of Sustainable Investing vs. Impact Investing

Sustainable Investments
There are several types of sustainable investments which are:

1. Socially Responsible Investing (SRI)

    Socially Responsible Investing is a type of investment that seeks to generate returns while doing something positive for the world. This might include promoting environmentally friendly practices or improving social mobility. SRI usually means investments in companies with positive social and environmental impacts.

    SRI has been growing in popularity in recent years. However, SRI has also attracted significant criticism and legal disputes, particularly in the United States. As I mentioned earlier, projects must be economically rational. And SRI has been signaled out for ignoring projects that are more likely to yield higher returns.

2. Ethical Investing

    Ethical investing is a philosophy that uses investment principles to uphold specific moral or ethical values. Ethical investors avoid companies that could negatively impact the environment and society. This is called negative screening, where investors exclude certain companies from their investment portfolio.

Chapter 2 - Sustainability and Impact Investing

For instance, investors might avoid companies involved in:

- Gambling, alcohol, and smoking,
- Animal testing,
- Weaponry and firearms,
- Oil and gas harvesting and more.

3. <u>Green Investing</u>

    Green investing focuses on environmentally friendly investments which includes:

    - Purchasing stocks in companies that use sustainable practices,
    - Renewable Energy projects
    - Waste reclamation
    - Water purification and reclamation

4. <u>Impact Investing</u>
    As we've seen, impact investing helps to create suitable vehicles for helping achieve sustainability. It offers capital programs to investors looking for better reasons than profit alone.

    Investors seek to put their money to make a difference and generate returns as well. The idea is to finance socially and environmentally-motivated companies.

Impact Investors invest in companies that impact education, healthcare, infrastructure, food & agriculture, green energy, social ventures, etc.

Investors who pursue value-based strategies try to find high-quality stocks undervalued by the market.

Types of Impact Investments

There are many types of impact investments, but a few of the most common are:

1. Social Impact Investing (SII)

SII focuses on solving social or environmental problems. They do so by investing in companies or projects that can make a positive impact.

SII investors seek to identify, fund, and grow companies that generate positive social and environmental effects. But, they also look at high-quality returns.

Chapter 2 - Sustainability and Impact Investing

2. <u>Environmental Impact Investing</u>

This investment approach focuses on reducing environmental impact or improving environmental sustainability in companies or projects. Environmental impact investing (EII) is a financial model that aims to generate positive social and ecological returns.

Generally, it does so by driving innovation in sustainable practices while improving the financial performance of investors. It combines the power of capital markets with sustainability concerns to achieve broad-based, systemic change.

EII (environmental impact investing) has emerged as an essential tool for investors and institutions. It helps them to identify, evaluate, and invest in opportunities that create environmental or social benefits. Funds based on EII focus on identifying start-up and mature companies where potential investment returns are tied to the impact of a project or business process.

3. <u>Community Development Impact Investing</u>

This investment supports economic growth by building and improving local communities. Community development impacts investors, who can be individuals or organizations. They also invest in companies or projects to impact communities positively.

By doing so, they can help to improve the quality of life for people in those communities while also making money. Development impact investing can be an effective way to generate financial returns and support social good.

4. <u>Ethical Investing</u>

Ethical Investing is a type of investment that aligns with ethical principles. This can include investing in companies that operate responsibly, employing people fairly, and helping reduce poverty rates.

There are many ethical considerations when investing. This can be very subjective as different people have different values and beliefs about what constitutes an ethical investment.

Chapter 2 - Sustainability and Impact Investing

Some common factors to consider are:
- The company's social and environmental impact,
- The effects of their operations on workers' rights and
- How well they treat local communities where they operate,
- Quality of issues surrounding human trafficking in supply chains or child labor as product components.
- health, whether they pay a fair wage to employees (including benefits like maternity leave),
-

Sustainable Investing Examples

Sustainable investing is a diversified investment approach. It seeks to help investors reduce environmental and social risk and improve long-term financial performance.

Sustainable Investing

Examples of sustainable investing include:

- Investing in companies that have a strong environmental or social impact.

- Buying stocks of companies using renewable energy sources, such as wind power and solar panels.

- Investing in companies that use natural resources efficiently, such as those that recycle or reuse materials.

- Invest in companies with high ethical, social, and environmental standards.

- Creating a portfolio of companies with substantial environmental, social, and governance (ESG) policies.

- Investing in companies that are developing or transitioning to more sustainable production methods.

- Diversifying your wealth across asset classes to mitigate potential volatility and increase stability.

- Diversifying your portfolio across asset classes to minimize possible fluctuations and create balance.

- Investing in companies that are developing or transitioning to more sustainable production methods.

Impact Investing Examples

There are several ways that investing can positively impact the world. Below are just a few examples:
- Investing in companies that create environmental sustainability initiatives

- Supporting social entrepreneurship

- Making donations

- Investing in renewable energy initiatives

This can help to provide:

- Better healthcare,

- Improve education,

- Promote agriculture for food security.

Sustainable Investing vs. Impact Investing Pros & Cons

What are the Pros and Cons of Sustainable Investing?

- risks.

Pros

- Helping to mitigate environmental, social, and economic It helps you make money while impacting the planet positively

Cons

- Lack of consensus over what constitutes a sustainable investment,
- Lack of transparency in the sustainable investment market.

What are the Pros and Cons of Impact Investing?

Pros
- Help solve social and environmental problems,
- Generate financial returns for investors, and
- Promote corporation responsibility

Cons

- It is challenging to identify which projects will have the most significant impact,
- There is a risk of losing money on investments,
- It can be challenging to penetrate the market.

Sustainable and Impact Investing are great ideas whose time has come. Europe is far ahead of the United States when it comes to sustainable investing but we are starting to catch up. There has been a negative publicity revolving around the fact that many of these projects have not been successful. But it goes back to what I said earlier, projects must make economic

sense. Many of you have undoubtedly seen the movie, *'Field of Dreams'* with Keven Costner. In it, the voice told him, *"If you build it, they will come."* Sadly, in the world of Sustainable Investing, that is not true. If you build it, investors will only come if they can make a comparable or superior return to a project with no social benefit.

CHAPTER 3

ESG Investing

"Don't let the fear of striking out hold you back"

~ **Babe Ruth**

ESG is a new style of investing that enhances the value of investments by taking full account of environmental, social and governance factors. That includes understanding the environmental, social and governance risks and opportunities they present – and how these could affect longer-term performance.

ESG means evaluating investments by how they are managing their strengths and weaknesses – whether related to climate change, human capital management, supply chain issues, diversity, or other balance sheet issues. The companies that score highest are the ones who promote or live best practice. Sustainability-driven approach expertise is applied to a wide range of specialist strategies to meet clients' specific ethical, socially responsible, and thematic (e.g., climate-based) investment goals. up for further updates on our breadth

ESG focuses on sustainability, resource efficiency and socio-economic benefit. By making ESG central to investment capabilities, you can deliver strong outcomes for investors as well as actively contribute to a fairer, more sustainable world.

More on what exactly is ESG?

ESG Investing is a term that is often used synonymously with sustainable investing, socially responsible investing, mission-related investing, or screening. It as the consideration of environmental, social and governance factors alongside financial factors in the investment decision-making process.

Under the ESG investing umbrella, three common investor objectives or motivations when considering an ESG strategy: Integration, Values, and Impact. In order to achieve these objectives, institutional investors may pursue different approaches such as ESG integration, exclusionary or negative screening, or thematic investing, to name a few.

Investors may consider several different ESG factors, metrics and data when looking to adopt an ESG investing strategy or apply ESG across a portfolio. These factors typically include industry-specific key issues such as climate change, human capital and labor management, corporate governance, gender diversity, privacy, and data security, among others. A mining company and a financial company, for example, may be faced with different key ESG risks and opportunities and therefore evaluated on the key issues specific to their respective industries.

The Evolution of ESG Investing

ESG is growing in significance amongst both institutional and retail investors. The practice of ESG investing began in the 1960s as socially responsible investing, with investors excluding stocks or entire industries from their portfolios based on business activities such as tobacco production or involvement in the South African apartheid regime.

Today, ethical considerations and alignment with values remain common motivations of many ESG investors but the field is rapidly growing and evolving, as investors look to incorporate ESG factors into the investment process alongside traditional financial analysis.

What are ESG rankings?

E, S, and G represent the three main pillars used to evaluate the "social responsibility" of companies.

Environmental
- Climate Change
- Renewable Energy

- Sustainability

Social

- Diversity
- Labor Relations
- Conflict Minerals

Governance

- Management Structure
- Board Independence
- Executive Compensation

There is no global standard for evaluating ESG metrics, but some third-party firms have established ranking methodologies. Personal Capital chooses to partner with Sustainalytics, a global leader in ESG research and ratings.

How Do ESG Rating Agencies Work – And Why Should You Care?

If you are a socially-conscious investor, you may wonder who determines which companies are deemed "socially responsible" and what criteria is used. After all, one person's view of social responsibility often differs radically from another person's view. Socially responsible investing is a broad, often subjective, notion, so can it be objectively evaluated?

Enormous interest in [socially responsible investing (SRI)](#) by both individual and institutional investors gave rise to a relatively young, but fast growing, industry—environmental, social, and governance (ESG) ratings agencies. Today, there are a handful of established agencies using rigorous criteria to evaluate companies based on ESG metrics.

How Do ESG Ratings Work?

While each agency has its own specific approach, the overall broad framework evaluates a company's "social responsibility" within these pillars:

- Environmental: Covers issues such as climate change, renewable energy, and sustainability
- Social: Covers issues like diversity, labor relations, and conflict minerals

- Governance: Covers matters such as management structure, board independence and executive compensation

The ratings process works much like company credit-rating agencies, such as Moody's or Standard & Poor's. These agencies rank companies based on financial factors. Results from credit agencies tend to be closely aligned, largely because the metrics they use are similar & well-defined.

ESG agencies, on the other hand, work with a host of non-financial data that cannot be delineated in the same manner as a more straightforward financial analysis. This means they work with less well-defined criteria, so scores for a single company can sometimes vary between agencies. ESG scoring is an evolving discipline — adopting a common language and reporting requirements are part of that ongoing process. However, it will likely be some time before there is any structured global methodology. The key, if you are looking for an ESG ratings firm, is to find a credible company with a robust research process you understand.

Sustainalytics: An Example

To illustrate the basic process, let us look at one agency's approach to ESG ratings, Sustainalytics which is an established global leader in ESG research and has a ratings history spanning more than 25 years. The agency serves more than 450 clients and has offices in 14 cities around the world.

Environmental, Social, and Governance (ESG) Investing. ESG investing is profiting from social, environmental, and governance considerations. These have become increasingly important in investment decisions. Generally, it involves investing in companies or assets that meet specific minimum standards for ESG performance.

There are many different ways to measure ESG performance. Some of the key factors include:

- Reducing greenhouse gas emissions,
- Improving employee and community well-being,
- Complying with ethical standards (e.g., human rights, environmental and consumer protection),
- Maintaining independence from political pressures or business risks to make informed decisions.

Chapter 3 – ESG Investing

In making their assessments, Sustainalytics evaluates ESG characteristics based on three key indicators, including:

- Preparedness: Assessments of company management systems and policies designed to manage material ESG issues.
- Disclosure: Assessments of whether company reporting meets international best-practice standards and is transparent with respect to most material ESG issues.
- Performance (both quantitative and qualitative): Assessments of company ESG performance based on quantitative metrics, such as carbon intensity; and qualitative assessments of company ESG performance based on the analysis of controversial incidents involving that company.

Sustainalytics covers approximately 11,000 companies across the globe and employs more than 170 researchers.

According to the company's website, *"An ESG report for a single company includes qualitative analysis and commentary on the company's ability to manage ESG issues; a summary of a company's ESG performance with environmental, social and governance scores in relation to industry peers; and an overview of any ESG controversies, with access to a full controversy report."*

Sustainalytics uses metrics, as well as direct engagement with companies, which allows for feedback and a greater ability to assess transparency with respect to ESG issues. This process produces an ESG score, which investors can use to make decisions relative to their objectives.

Why Should an Investor Care About ESG Ratings?

Ratings agencies provide lots of additional analysis, and more information is always better. In fact, evidence indicates that ratings agencies help accomplish some of the social goals of ESG-conscious investors. For example, scoring helps motivate companies to create, adhere to, and disclose their ESG policies. And putting ESG issues on the radar for leadership at every company is part of the

mission for many socially responsible investors.

Chapter 3 – ESG Investing

Take Away

Correctly measuring socially responsible success starts with fully understanding how the securities in your portfolio were chosen and how they will be monitored going forward. ESG research and ranking metrics are used to help create a socially responsible plan. But ESG scores are just a piece of the overall equation—you still need to figure out how to apply them in your portfolio. It is best to use your own vetting process—taking a "best in class" approach to the US equity component of portfolios by removing all companies with ESG scores below their peer group average, and subsequently apply a smart weighting methodology to the remaining universe. Smart Weighting is an investment approach that more evenly
weights the factors of size, style, and sector when compared to traditional cap-weighted indices. We then attempt to choose companies with the highest overall ESG scores. On average, our chosen US stocks have ESG scores above the 90th percentile relative to their domestic counterparts.

How ESG Metrics Work and why all investors should care?

What are ESG Metrics, what do they measure and how good are they have measures of ESG stands for

Environmental, Social and Governance. And what that really is, is a framework for analyzing companies and really assessing how are they compared to their peers in terms of performance against these metrics, and the E, you have for environmentally have a water usage, waste, production, and general kind of environmental behavior, how efficient they are and managing their resources and looking at the environment around them. Under social, it is about how would they treat their clients, how do they treat their workers, and then there also some diversity aspects around the management the workforce. Under Governance, the focus is around share class structure and governance structure within the company, how well run is the company and when you take it all together, you are looking at another way of assessing a company to see how it impacts the broader society at large.

How well do these metrics measure what they are supposed to be measuring and where do they fall short? In general, ESG metrics do a good job in direct company comparisons, but it is less good. I think we are looking at what is the overall mission of a company in terms of is it our best do good? And if so, how do you how do you manage that? I think the other way where it kind of falls a little bit short, it is a little bit of a framework. So, lots of people have different

Chapter 3 – ESG Investing

views   around   what   is   more

important for some people it is around environmental is more important, but others it is social governance, you know, as many people as there are in a room, there are going to be different opinions as to what actually is important. And so, unless you are going to go and build a bespoke portfolio for someone in a separately managed account, there is going to be some degree of compromise around how that ESG framework is going to be applied.

Are they self-reported or companies sharing these metrics with investors at large?

Most of the data is public. It is a combination of self-reported, and also analysis done by analysts who are pouring over company fact sheets, you know, the regulatory reporting, and so forth. So, because of that, you do tend to get better reporting from larger companies but you can get reporting for companies all the way down to cap structure, cap size, and internationally as well, you know, we are able to produce an ESG framework that enables you to look at large cap value as well as small cap but also emerging markets in developed markets as well.

What advice would you give to people who want to invest along their values and who maybe have not spent a lot of

time looking at the ESG metrics, what is some way to get them over the hurdle where it feels like there is just too many?

There are a couple of things they are going to have to define for themselves. There are certain ESG providers that have a very specific slant to how they are doing it. And they must decide whether that is what they are looking for, whether it is based on religious or certain other social aspects, if they are looking for just general ESG and in terms of framework for companies that are better stewards of the environment, social, then you really, they should either look for ESG providers. There are certain companies that have been in the space for a long time and all ESG funds will be labeled ESG or responsible investing or impact because if you have any ESG fund, you are going to put that in the name somewhere and then you need to look at how the products work. Look at the criteria by which companies are being scored, that should be very clear and apparent within the fund's literature. If it is not, maybe they move on to another provider. If you are looking at your retirement plan, maybe talk to whoever runs your company's retirement plan and ask them about responsible investing options for that plan.

Can you still make money and investment responsibly?

So historically, the knock has been that to have socially conscious investing you will have to compromise your performance expectations. That is clearly not the case. In fact, for many years when technology companies led the pack it was the opposite. But the point is that using an ESG framework can actually help you avoid companies with bad practices. And for example, when we had the Equifax scandal, Equifax had actually been downgraded by major ESG data providers over data privacy and security issues about 18 months to two years beforehand. You know, within our large cap growth ETF, Facebook had not been included, because it is scored relatively poorly compared to other tech companies over data privacy concerns.

Something that needs to be considered as part of the ESG framework is data privacy. As it is very important to a lot of people, many have divesting from Facebook or Meta.

So, you know, when you are looking at a company like the data provider score and the company so we use MSCI as our data provider, when they score the company, they score it based on all the different criteria, and under social data privacy is in there. So, when you are looking at controversial business practices which is another way of scoring companies, you look at things that could be controversial. And so, the data privacy issue had come up from the 2014 kind of conversation we had with the government. So, that was something was always on the radar. And so, Facebook/ Metta does not have a particularly bad ESG score on absolute terms but compared to the rest of the tech sector, which tends to do better, it scored relatively poorly. So, within our large cap growth, ETF right, it scored poorly in tech, it did not make the cut off the tech, so we did not have it in there. So, you know, last year as Facebook did quite well, our performance suffered this year, with our Facebook in their performance has done quite well.

Is Divesting a good way for investors to express their values?

So, divestment is one tactic you can use I think, you know, we have certain industries where we do diversify from so weapons manufacturers, alcohol, gambling, tobacco, and then nuclear power. However, those are industries that we feel that like they are essentially, they are putting that in stock basket and so we diverse beyond that I think if you are just doing straight divesting, what you are doing is taking yourself out of the conversation with the company with the issue of the stock. For example, if you were to divest from energy companies, you could not actually be in a conversation with them as a major shareholder encouraging them to look at, say renewables, right. So, you need to weigh up diversity, which is where I feel good because I am not invested in what I think is a sane stock versus what I have no say in trying to influence that company's behavior. So, it can be a little bit self-defeating, because you have now removed yourself from that conversation with the company.

How much does it cost to be socially responsible investor and are the fees higher?

Fees are not higher on socially responsible investments. Most of these are large cap companies that you know the names. They are part of the S&P 500. Someone once said, to me, it is very much like non-financial quality factors you can look at ESG is almost like a smart beta overlay, particularly when you consider the risk management aspects of it. We put together a series of portfolios using all the building blocks within our ESG ETF suite and it came in most of the time under 30 basis points.

So, investors can invest according to their beliefs without paying extra to do so.

Well, if you think about the factors themselves, they are effectively, how well run is the companies, you should be looking at quality factors, right? And quality is one of the more nebulous of the smart beta major factors and so you could say, this is just another way of defining quality in the company. Does it waste resources, does it look after its customers and get it stay out of trouble with the regulators? Does it have a decent management structure that encourages accountability? So, by having that framework in place you can avoid companies like Volkswagen or BP before the Deepwater Horizon incident had been downgraded and removed from major ESG indices over concerns about the outsourcing of maintenance of offshore oil wells which is precisely what happened there. So, it is really a very good risk management tool. MSCI does research and found that companies in the bottom 10% for ESG score had a much higher likelihood of what they deemed to be a catastrophic or material drop in share price a from an incident by material they were talking 90%.

And so, by having this framework in place, you are really putting in place a method for trying to avoid tail risk from companies that are badly run and may end up having serious, serious scandals in the press.

CHAPTER 4

Climate Tech and Decarbonization

"Unless someone like you cares a whole awful lot, nothing is going to get better. It's not"

~ Dr. Seuss

Post COP 28, the world is entering into a new phase to decarbonize the planet. The goal is to reach a zero-carbon footprint by 2050. The investment community is clamoring to figure out how to generate superior risk by opportunities arising from the transition to a sustainable & decarbonized global economy.

Sustainability

Sustainable investing can be described as is directing capital to companies that seek to combat climate change, while promoting social and corporate responsibility. As discussed previously, Environmental, Social and

Chapter 4 – Climate Tech

Governance (ESG) refers to three important factors in measuring sustainability:

- Environmental criteria look at a company's impact on our planet (climate change, pollution, resource depletion, etc.)
- Social criteria access a company's relationship with its employees, customers, and communities (working conditions, health and safety, diversity, etc.)
- Governance examines a company's quality of management (leadership, internal controls, shareholder rights, audits, corruption, etc.)

Sustainable investing involves integrating ESG information into investment decision making process. One specific type of impact or ESG involves Decarbonization for Climate Tech. I like to use the acronym W.A.F.E, Water, Air, Food and Energy to describe the focus of Climate Tech.

What is Decarbonization?

As we defined in the first chapter, decarbonization is the reduction or elimination of carbon dioxide emissions from a process such as manufacturing or the production of energy.

To keep the planet from warming more than 1.5°C above pre-industrial levels, most countries, including the U.S., have goals to reach net zero by 2050. Net zero means that all greenhouse gas emissions produced are counterbalanced by an equal amount of emissions that are eliminated. Achieving this will require rapid decarbonization.

There are two aspects to decarbonization. The first entails reducing the greenhouse gas emissions produced by the combustion of fossil fuels. This can be done by preventing emissions using zero-carbon renewable energy sources such as wind, solar, hydropower, geothermal and biomass, which now make up one-third of global power capacity, and electrifying as many sectors as possible. Energy efficiency will reduce the demand for energy, but increasing electrification

Chapter 4 – Climate Tech

will increase it, and in 2050, the demand for power is expected to be more than double what it is today.

Consequently, decarbonization will also require absorbing carbon from the atmosphere by capturing emissions and enhancing carbon storage in agricultural lands and forests.

To achieve decarbonization, all aspects of the economy must change—from how energy is generated, and how we produce and deliver goods and services, to how lands are managed. The carbon dioxide and methane emissions that are warming the planet come are mostly related to energy. The are from the power generation by industry, transport, buildings, and agriculture and land use sectors of the global economy, so these sectors must all be transformed. The following is what decarbonization could look like in each sector.

Power generation

With the global population expected to reach 10 billion in 2060, and increasing electrification of society, the demand for electricity will grow, so decreasing the emissions per unit of electricity produced is essential. Power generation, including electricity and heat production, is responsible for 30 percent of global CO_2 emissions because of the fossil fuels involved; they need to be replaced by renewable energy.

Renewable sources are now so economical that they made up the majority of new energy generation capacity in 2018. Solar energy prices have dropped about 80 percent in the last 10 years, while wind power has fallen 40 percent. Utility scale battery storage costs dropped 70 percent between 2015 and 2018. However, because renewable energy sources are intermittent, utilities still rely on the consistent baseline energy that fossil fuel and nuclear power plants can provide.

For the U.S. to reach its net zero goal, it must go from generating about 20 percent of electricity from carbon-free sources today to at least 75 percent by 2030. This will require increasing renewable energy generation and maintaining nuclear energy sources if the nuclear power plants are safe. Coal plants must be retired or retrofitted to capture 90 percent of their emissions. Carbon capture, utilization and storage needs to be expanded to capture CO_2 emissions from remaining fossil fuel power plants. This CO_2 can be

Chapter 4 – Climate Tech

used onsite or transported elsewhere for use in fuels, chemicals, or building materials, or injected into an underground reservoir for permanent storage.

Power plants must also be made more energy efficient. Two-thirds of the energy consumed to produce electricity is lost as waste heat; using that waste heat to warm the plant or nearby buildings, for example, can increase the energy efficiency of power generation by 80 percent.

Transmission lines must be built out to take renewable energy from where it is generated to all parts of the country. As renewables are increasingly integrated into the grid, improved low-cost energy storage for the grid is needed to help smooth out their intermittency and ensure dependability, especially as climate change brings more extreme weather.

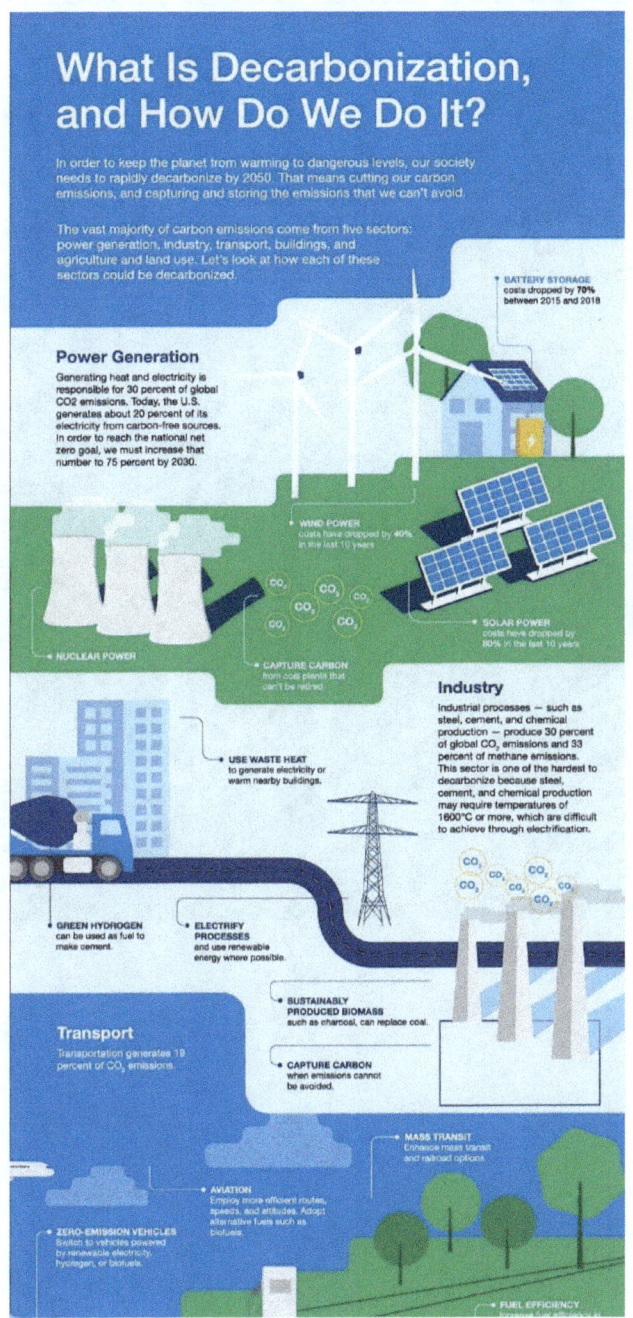

Chapter 4 – Climate Tech

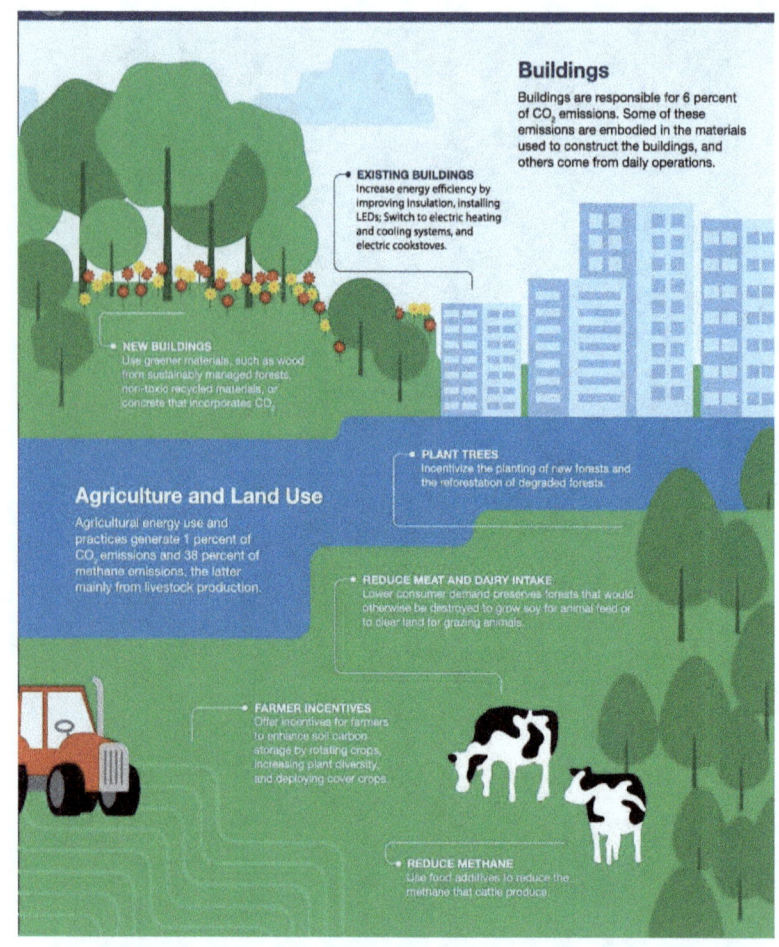

Growth in Sustainability Investing

Demand for ESG investing from institutional and individual investors is driving money managers to incorporate ESG in their investment process. Major pension plans (i.e., CalPERS, CalSTRS, NY Commons, etc.) are directing more assets to investment strategies that incorporate ESG. Currently only ¼ of all assets under management are in sustainable investment strategies. Millennials and women will account for 75% of the labor force in 2025. These two demographics are highly concerned about climate change, thus most of their savings will go toward sustainability investing.

Is now the time for Sustainable Investing? Below is an Executive Action from the California Governor Newsom directing California as the state transitions to a carbon- neutral economy to transition to a carbon-neutral economy. To do so he is directing the California Pension Plans to invest accordingly.

So, this is quite an opportunity for investors. It is equivocal to investing in alcoholic beverage companies knowing that prohibition is about to end.

There are a lot of words associated with sustainability and climate change. Some of them are overused buzzwords, while others are meaningful descriptions of new technologies and policies that can help the planet. One of the strongest words associated with addressing global warming is decarbonization — but this word is also used to describe another process that has little to do with climate change, yet everything to do with creating more fuel-efficient vehicles.

How do we Implement a Decarbonization Strategy?

Decarbonization can mean two things: it can refer to moving away from energy systems that produce carbon dioxide (CO_2) and other greenhouse gas emissions, or it can refer to removing carbon buildup and carbon deposits from internal combustion engines. While both processes involve removing carbon, they do it in very different ways.

Energy decarbonization involves shifting the entire energy system in an attempt to stop carbon emissions from entering the atmosphere before they are ever released — and part of that process also involves using carbon capture technologies to remove CO2 from the air after it has already been released. This involves decarbonizing power grids, decarbonizing supply chains, and utilizing carbon sequestration in the pursuit of net-zero emissions and a carbon-neutral global economy.

Engine decarbonization is much different, and it involves removing built-up carbon residue that accumulates in internal combustion engines from fossil fuels that release carbon when they are burned.

What Does it Mean to Decarbonize Electricity?

The bottom line is that regardless of what resources are used, decarbonization of electricity entails moving away from energy usage and other processes that emit the most common [greenhouse gas (GHG)](): carbon dioxide.

[Electrification is the best energy transition path]() we currently have to try and keep in line with the Paris climate agreement goals. Not only is this easily integrated with global economic sectors, but it is also cost-effective, and most importantly, we know it works. However, with electrification comes increased demand for electricity — which means significantly more

Chapter 4 – Climate Tech

electricity generation is needed. In fact, some people predict that we will need twice as much electricity to cover full-scale electrification of the global economy.

Decarbonizing our current worldwide electricity generation is a difficult challenge — needing to not only get to 100% of current capacity with renewable energy but also to reach three times the current level. That is why true decarbonization of our electrical grid and energy systems cannot rely on renewables alone. Every form of alternative energy, from small-scale nuclear power to methanol to all forms of hydrogen need to be utilized to get us to the point where carbon emissions are reduced to nothing and we reach a net- zero carbon world.

Decarbonization in the Future

As we move toward a more [carbon-neutral](#) global economy, and greenhouse gas emissions are continually reduced in all aspects of society, engine decarbonization will become less needed. More and more people are switching to electric vehicles each year, which do not require decarbonizing at all, and modern internal combustion engines are seeing less carbon buildup as fuel efficiency continues to increase and carbon residue in fuels continues to decrease.

Decarbonizing electricity and energy usage is a complicated challenge that will require a global effort to achieve. This will involve deep decarbonization, utilizing out-of-the-box energy resources and creating entirely different systems for how we generate and consume not just electricity but also energy in general.

The Earth has been on a consistent warming trend since the 19th century. During this time, the surface temperature has risen roughly 2 degrees Fahrenheit. This has resulted in rising sea levels, which has displaced people and wildlife in low- lying areas, and severe weather patterns that have caused droughts, flooding, severe storms, and even wildfires.

In an attempt to slow climate change, the United Nations (U.N.) has stepped in and brought a collection of the world's countries together in a concerted effort to lower global emissions to net zero by 2050. Unfortunately, the world is falling short on emissions goals to date.

Chapter 4 – Climate Tech

What Is the United Nations' Stance on Climate Change?

The United Nations has long had a stance on slowing climate change and hopefully reversing its impact on the world over time. In 2015, it struck a landmark agreement to combat climate change among parties to the United Nations Framework Convention on Climate Change (UNFCCC) at the 21st Conference of the Parties (COP21) in Paris.

More commonly known as The Paris Agreement, this accord's goal was to strengthen the world's response to the threat of climate change. It aimed to do so by holding this century's global temperature increase to below 2 degrees Celsius above pre-industrial levels. It also aimed to keep the temperature rise at 1.5 degrees Celsius or lower.

On April 22, 2016, Earth Day, 175 members of the U.N. signed The Paris Agreement. As of 2023, 194 countries in total have ratified the agreements.

What Climate Change Action Was Taken at COP27?

At the 27th Conference of the Parties (COP27), which took place November 6 through November 20, 2022, climate change and global warming were front and center once again. At this conference, the landmark deal reached was to establish the "loss and damage" fund. This fund would help vulnerable countries that undergo severe damage or loss due to climate disasters.

COP27 also saw many climate-focused decisions, but the Sharm el-Sheikh Implementation Plan was the cover decision. This plan highlights that becoming a low-carbon economy will require a $4 trillion to $6 trillion investment annually. To deliver this kind of funding, the world needs to swiftly and comprehensively update the financial system's structures and processes.

That wasn't the only climate-focused decision made at COP27. Others included:
- Sharm El-Sheikh joint work on implementation of climate

  action on agriculture and food security
- Implementation of the Global Climate Observing System

Chapter 4 – Climate Tech

- Common metrics used to calculate the carbon dioxide equivalence of anthropogenic greenhouse gas emissions by sources and removals by sinks
- Matters relating to Action for Climate Empowerment
- Long-term climate finance
- Report of the Green Climate Fund to the Conference of the Parties and guidance to the Green Climate Fund

What Does Net Zero by 2050 Mean?

The Paris Agreement's goal of keeping global warming at or below 1.5 degrees Celsius for the century is only possible if global emissions drop 45% by 2030 and we attain true net zero by 2050. Net zero by 2050 means the world has completely changed how it produces, consumes, and moves about in a way that produces zero greenhouse gas (GHG) emissions.

Fossil Fuel Usage accounts for a whopping 75% of the GHG emissions today, making it a focal point to avoiding some of the most significant impacts of climate change. The goal is to eliminate fossil-fuel power and replace it with renewable energy, such as solar or wind.

Sadly, the world is not on pace to meet the goal of being net zero by 2050. According to the U.N., the national climate plans of the 193 Parties to The Paris Agreement would result in a nearly 11% increase in GHG emissions by 2030 relative to 2010 levels. We're going in reverse, despite The Paris Agreement.

At COP26, the U.N. looked to right the ship with the Glasgow Climate Pact, which the U.N. says "completes the Paris rulebook." The Glasgow Pact aims to continue driving action on key points, including:

- Mitigation: Lower greenhouse gas emissions
- Adaptation: Providing aid to those impacted by climate change
- Finance: Giving countries access to the funds needed to attain their climate change goals
- Collaboration: Working in unison toward the common goal of slowing climate change

What Is the Leading Cause of Climate Change?

Many things can lead to climate change, but the U.N. points toward one group that has the largest impact: fossil fuels. This includes coal, oil, and natural gas. According to the U.N., these are "by far the largest contributor to global climate change." They account for three-quarters of the

Chapter 4 – Climate Tech

GHG emissions worldwide and about 90% of all carbon dioxide emissions.

These fossil fuels play pivotal roles in our daily lives, making them relatively difficult just to stop using. They play a role in our power generation, manufacturing operations, daily transportation and shipping, food production, and more. Add to that unsustainable development that results in deforestation, which eliminates valuable carbon sinks — objects that absorb carbon from the atmosphere — and the issues are compounded.

What Happened with Climate Change 2023?

Climate change did not improve in 2023. In fact, January 2023 was the seventh-warmest January recorded in 174 years. Also, there is a 99% chance that 2023 will be among the top 10 warmest years on record. Those are not promising signs for our fight against climate change.

These rising temperatures also resulted in record-low sea ice. According to data, the sea ice extent was lower than the previous record low in 2017 by 210,000 square miles.

Which are the Top 3 Countries Contributing to Climate Change?

You can view countries and their contribution to climate change in two ways: overall GHG emissions and GHG emissions per capita. In overall emissions, the top three contributors to climate change are:
- China at 12.7 billion metric tons of carbon dioxide equivalent (MtCO2e)
- The United States at 6 billion MtCO2e
- India at 3.4 billion MtCO2e

However, considering these are also three of the most populated countries in the world, that tends to skew the emissions numbers. Per capita — meaning per person — the three biggest GHG emitters in the world are much different. They are:
- Qatar at 35.59 metric tons
- Bahrain at 26.66 metric tons
- Kuwait at 24.97 metric tons

The U.S. comes in at number 12 on the per-capita list.

Chapter 4 - -Climate Tech

Sources of Greenhouse Gas Emissions

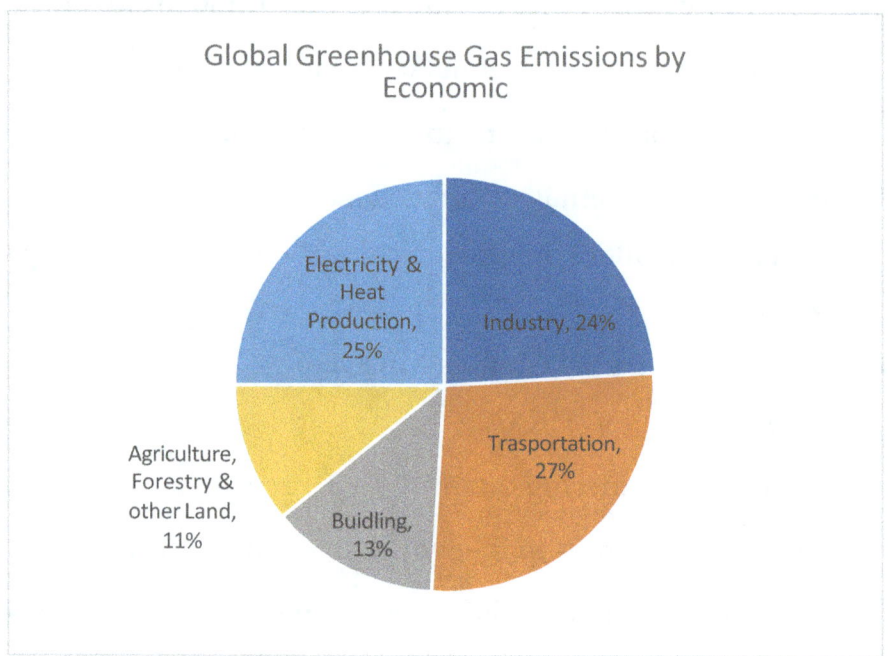

Total Emissions in 2020 = 5,981 <u>Million Metric Tons of CO2 equivalent</u>. Percentages may not add up to 100% due to independent rounding.

* Land Use, Land-Use Change, and Forestry in the United States is a net sink and removes approximately 13% of these greenhouse gas emissions. This net sink is not shown in the above diagram. All emission estimates from the

Greenhouse gases trap heat and make the planet warmer. Human activities are responsible for almost all of the increase in greenhouse gases in the atmosphere over the last 150 years.[1] The largest source of greenhouse gas emissions from human activities in the United States is from burning fossil fuels for electricity, heat, and transportation.

EPA tracks total U.S. emissions by publishing the *Inventory of U.S. Greenhouse Gas Emissions and Sinks*. This annual report estimates the total national greenhouse gas emissions and removals associated with human activities across the United States.

The primary sources of greenhouse gas emissions in the United States are:

- Transportation (27% of 2020 greenhouse gas emissions) – The transportation sector generates the largest share of greenhouse gas emissions. Greenhouse gas emissions from transportation primarily come from burning fossil fuel for our cars, trucks, ships, trains, and planes. Over 90% of the fuel used for transportation is petroleum based, which includes primarily gasoline and diesel.

- Electricity production (25% of 2020 greenhouse gas emissions) – Electric power generates the second largest share of greenhouse gas emissions. Approximately 60% of our electricity comes from burning fossil fuels, mostly coal and natural gas.[3]

- Industry (24% of 2020 greenhouse gas emissions) – Greenhouse gas emissions from industry primarily come from burning fossil fuels, as well as greenhouse gas emissions from certain chemical reactions necessary to produce goods from raw materials.

- Commercial and Residential (13% of 2020 greenhouse gas emissions) – Greenhouse gas emissions from businesses and homes arise primarily from fossil fuels burned for heat, the use of certain products that contain greenhouse gases, and the handling of waste.

- Agriculture (11% of 2020 greenhouse gas emissions) – Greenhouse gas emissions from agriculture come from livestock, agricultural soils, and rice production.

- Land Use and Forestry (13% of 2020 greenhouse gas emissions) – Land areas can act as a sink (absorbing CO_2 from the atmosphere) or a source of greenhouse gas emissions. In the U.S., since 1990, managed forests and other lands are a net sink, i.e., they have absorbed more CO_2 from the atmosphere than they emit.

- Emissions and Trends

    Since 1990, gross U.S. greenhouse gas emissions have decreased by 7%. From year to year, emissions can rise and fall due to changes in the economy, the price of fuel, and other factors. In 2020, U.S. greenhouse gas emissions decreased 11% compared to 2019 levels. The sharp decline in emissions was primarily from CO_2 emissions from fossil fuel combustion and was largely due to the coronavirus (COVID-19) pandemic-related reductions in travel and economic activity, including a 13% decrease in transportation emissions driven by less travel due to the COVID-19 pandemic. Electric power sector emissions decreased 10% due to a slight decrease in electricity demand from the COVID-19 pandemic and a continued shift from coal to less carbon-intensive natural gas and renewables.

Calif. Gov. Newsom Announces Executive Action to Leverage State's Pension Investments, Transportation Systems to Strengthen Climate Resiliency

SACRAMENTO, California, Sept. 20, 2019 -- Gov. Gavin Newsom, D-California, issued the following news release:

* * *

- Governor directs Department of Finance to create a Climate Investment Framework to leverage the state's $700 billion CalPERS, CalSTRS and UC Retirement Program portfolio to drive investment toward carbon-neutral technologies

- Governor Newsom also signs legislation strengthening the state's emissions standards and establishing the nation's first "smog check" for diesel trucks

* * *

Just days before global leaders converge in New York City for Climate Week and months after California struck a major agreement with four automakers on vehicle emission standards, Governor Gavin Newsom today signed a landmark executive order to leverage the state's $700 billion pension investment portfolio and assets to advance California's climate leadership. The executive order also directs multiple state agencies and departments to review and update overall operations, transportation investments, and use of the state's purchasing power to advance groundbreaking climate goals.

The Governor also signed two important bills today to strengthen emission standards for trucks, semis, and other high-pollution vehicles. SB 210 by Senator Connie Leyva (D- Chino) requires the California Air Resources Board (CARB) to develop and implement a Heavy-Duty Inspection and Maintenance Program for non-gasoline, heavy-duty trucks -- the first 'smog check' program of its kind in the nation. SB 44 by Senator Nancy Skinner (D-Berkeley) requires CARB to create a comprehensive plan for reducing greenhouse gas emissions from medium and heavy-duty vehicles. Medium and heavy-duty diesel trucks make up only four percent of the 28.2 million vehicles on the road in California but accounted for 20 percent of greenhouse gas emissions from the transportation sector and 8 percent of statewide greenhouse gas emissions this year. Cars, trucks, and other vehicles are responsible for more than 80 percent of

Chapter 4 – Climate Tech

smog-forming pollution.

"In the face of the White House's inaction on climate change, California is stepping up and leading the way," said Governor Newsom. "Our state is proof that you can reach some of the strongest climate goals in the world while also achieving record economic growth. How we meet this moment will define our state - and country - for decades to come, just as the emergence of the internet defined our economy over the past few decades. We have to get ahead of this and align our state investments, our purchasing power and our transportation and housing policies to be ready to meet this moment head- on."

California is a global leader in climate change mitigation efforts through bold climate goals and actions, as well as leadership in the U.S. Climate Alliance and Under2 Coalition, using the state's power as the fifth largest economy in the world to drive positive action. California

has ambitious and essential climate goals to transition to a healthier, more sustainable, and more inclusive economy, including: reducing greenhouse gas emissions
40 percent below 1990 levels by 2030; providing 100 percent of the state's electricity from clean energy sources by 2045; reducing methane emissions and

Chapter 4 – Climate Tech

hydrofluorocarbon gases by 40 percent; and adding 5 million zero-emission vehicles to California's roads by 2030.

This executive order continues the Governor's commitment to strengthening California's resilience while investing in new technologies, programs, and best practices to lower carbon emissions. To mitigate climate threats to our communities and increase carbon sequestration, the Governor invested in forest health and fuel reduction and held utilities accountable for building resiliency. The Governor also directed state agencies to develop a comprehensive strategy to build a climate-resilient water system and made a historic investment to develop the workforce for California's future carbon-neutral economy.

The executive order will advance California's climate goals by leveraging:

State Investments: California has an investment portfolio of over $700 billion through CalPERS, CalSTRS, and the University of California Retirement System. As the state transitions to a carbon-neutral economy, and as other states and countries increasingly adopt ambitious climate policy, the state's investments must align with the reality of this major market shift. The Governor's executive order directs

Chapter 4 – Climate Tech

the Department of Finance to create a Climate Investment Framework to measure and manage climate risk across the state's investment portfolio, with the goal of driving investment toward carbon-neutral and climate resilient technologies. The Framework will provide a timeline and criteria to shift investments to companies and industry sectors that have greater growth potential based on their focus of adapting to and mitigating the impacts of climate change, including investments in carbon-neutral, carbon-negative, and clean energy technologies.

Transportation Systems: The California State

Transportation Agency (CalSTA) is directed to invest its annual portfolio of
$5 billion toward construction, operations, and maintenance to help reverse the trend of increased fuel consumption and reduce greenhouse gas emissions associated with the transportation sector. CalSTA, in consultation with the Department of Finance, is also directed to align transportation spending, programming, and mitigation with the state's climate goals to achieve the objectives of the state's Climate Change Scoping Plan, where feasible. Specifically, the Governor is ordering a focus for transportation investments near housing, and on managing congestion through innovative strategies that encourage alternatives to driving.

Chapter 4 – Climate Tech

State Assets and Operations: California owns and manages major physical assets through the Department of General Services (DGS), including 19 million square feet of buildings and over 51,000 vehicles. We are also a major purchaser of products across our agencies. As a global leader on climate change, and as a responsible asset owner and manager, we must lead by example in

our own state operations by aligning our operations with our values. As property owners and managers, we must take the physical impacts from a changing climate into account, as the private sector (bond raters and issuers, reinsurers, and insurers) is increasingly doing. With this executive order, the Governor is directing DGS to identify opportunities to lower emissions and mitigate climate risk from the state's owned and leased assets, primarily buildings and vehicles, and to implement sustainable purchasing

policies across state agencies that prioritize the purchase of environmentally preferable goods, consistent with state climate policies.

Vehicles and Electric Vehicle Infrastructure: Moving away from internal combustion engines is critical to reduce carbon emissions and to address major pollution issues across the state, especially in the Central Valley and Inland Empire. Through the executive order, the Governor directs

CARB to push automakers to produce even more clean vehicles, and to find ways for more Californians to purchase these vehicles on the new and used markets. CARB is tasked with developing new grant criteria for clean vehicle programs to encourage manufacturers to produce clean, affordable cars and propose new strategies to increase demand in the primary and secondary markets for zero emission vehicles. Finally, CARB shall strengthen existing or adopt new regulations to achieve greenhouse gas reductions within the transportation sector.

Governor Newsom will travel to New York City next week to participate in New York Climate Week events and discuss California's climate leadership in sustainability, clean energy, and fuel standards at the World Economic Forum.

A copy of today's executive order can be found here (https://www.gov.ca.gov/wp-content/uploads/2019/09/9.20.19-Climate-EO-N-19-19.pdf).

Chapter 4 – Climate Tech

www.ingramcontent.com/pod-product-compliance
Lightning Source LLC
Chambersburg PA
CBHW070200230526
45471CB00002B/745